ANIMAL KINGDOM CLASSIFICATION

ANT LIONS, WASPS & OTHER

INSECTS

By Steve Parker
Content Adviser: Debbie Folkerts, Ph.D.,
Assistant Professor of Biological Sciences,
Auburn University, Alabama

Science Adviser: Terrence E. Young Jr., M.Ed., M.L.S.,
Jefferson Parish (Louisiana) Public School System

First published in the United States in 2006 by
Compass Point Books
3109 West 50th Street #115
Minneapolis, MN 55410

ANIMAL KINGDOM CLASSIFICATION—INSECTS
was produced by

David West Children's Books
7 Princeton Court
55 Felsham Road
London SW15 1AZ

Designer: Gary Jeffrey
Editors: Gail Bushnell, Nadia Higgins
Page Production: Les Tranby, James Mackey

Visit Compass Point Books on the Internet at
www.compasspointbooks.com
or e-mail your request to
custserv@compasspointbooks.com

Library of Congress Cataloging-in-Publication Data
Parker, Steve.
   Ant lions, wasps, and other insects / by Steve Parker.
      p. cm.—(Animal kingdom classification)
   Includes bibliographical references and index.
   ISBN 0-7565-1250-6 (hardcover)
   1. Insects—Juvenile literature. I. Title. II. Series.
   QL467.2.P35195 2006
   595.7—dc22   2005003685

PHOTO CREDITS :
Abbreviations: t-top, m-middle, b-bottom, r-right,
l-left, c-center.

Pages 13t John Downer / naturepl.com; 16r, Dietmar Nill /
naturepl.com; 17t, Solvin Zankl / naturepl.com, 17l, Geoff Dore
/ naturepl.com; 18r, PREMAPHOTOS / naturepl.com; 19r, Hans
Christoph Kappel / naturepl.com; 20r, Ingo Arndt /
naturepl.com; 21cr, Doug Wechsler / naturepl.com; 22t, Doug
Wechsler / naturepl.com; 23r PREMAPHOTOS / naturepl.com;
25r, PREMAPHOTOS / naturepl.com, 25b, Duncan McEwan /
naturepl.com; 26t, Martin Dohrn / naturepl.com, 26l,
PREMAPHOTOS / naturepl.com; 27r, PREMAPHOTOS /
naturepl.com; 28r, Chris Packham / naturepl.com; 29t, Jose B.
Ruiz / naturepl.com, 29l, Hans Christoph Kappel / naturepl.com,
29r, Mike Wilkes / naturepl.com; 30c, DUNCAN McEWAN /
naturepl.com; page 31l, Adrian Davies / naturepl.com;
32c(main), Bruce Davidson / naturepl.com; 33t,
PREMAPHOTOS / naturepl.com; 34l, David Welling /
naturepl.com, 34r, Jeff Foott / naturepl.com; 35tr, John
Cancalosi / naturepl.com; 36t, PREMAPHOTOS / naturepl.com;
38t, Jose B. Ruiz / naturepl.com, 38l, Adrian Davies /
naturepl.com; 39t, Dietmar Nill / naturepl.com; 40t, Jose B. Ruiz
/ naturepl.com; 42bl, Peter Hansen, 42br, Linda Bucklin; 43l,
Niall Benvie / naturepl.com, 43r, Oxford Scientific Films; 45b,
Digital Vision.

Every effort has been made to contact copyright
holders of any material reproduced in this book.
Any omissions will be rectified in subsequent
printings if notice is given to the publishers.

Cover: beetle
Opposite: dragonfly nymph

ANIMAL KINGDOM CLASSIFICATION

ANT LIONS, WASPS & OTHER
INSECTS

Steve Parker

COMPASS POINT BOOKS ✦ MINNEAPOLIS, MINNESOTA

TABLE OF CONTENTS

INTRODUCTION

No other kinds of animals are so varied or so numerous or live in so many different habitats as insects. Only the open ocean lacks them. In a tropical forest, they form more than half the weight of all the living creatures there. A single swarm of locusts may contain more individuals than there are people on Earth.

Insects are the largest group in the animal kingdom. The number of different species is much greater than all the other kinds of animals combined. About 1 million different insect species have been described so far by scientists. Many more millions almost certainly wait to be discovered in remote forests, caves, and valleys.

ANT POWER

Some of the best-known insects are ants, and there are more than 9,000 species of them. In some regions, ants dig more soil than earthworms and eat more food than all the other animals put together. A single ant nest may house more than 1 million individuals.

INSECTS RULE!

Insects thrive in every land and freshwater habitat, from the tops of mountains to the driest deserts and fastest-flowing rivers. Some insects move easily between habitats. Others are restricted to one area and one food source, such as a single type of tree.

INSECT SUCCESS

Part of the reason for insects' success is the way they pass through four different stages of life. This is known as metamorphosis. Nearly all insects hatch from eggs. The egg cases can be so tough that they resist the harshest conditions, from being frozen to almost boiled.

An insect's whole life cycle can take place fast—in some cases, just a few weeks. Insects can breed so rapidly that they build up huge numbers in months. This is important because, in most habitats, insects are the main prey for all kinds of larger creatures. So insects need to breed quickly to replace those eaten and to keep up their population.

EVERY HABITAT

The fast life cycle has other benefits. In some habitats, conditions for breeding are suitable only briefly, such as during a rainfall in a desert. Insects there breed rapidly, then their tough eggs survive the long dry periods.

TEMPERATE FORESTS
Katydid

WETLANDS
Damselfly

OPEN WOODLANDS
Firebugs

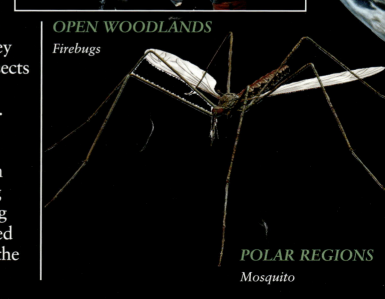

POLAR REGIONS
Mosquito

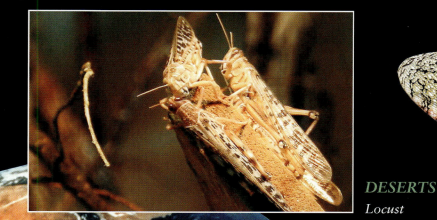

DESERTS
Locust

**GRASSLANDS
AND BUSH**
Dung beetle

INSECTS TO AVOID

In most habitats there are a few insects that are dangerous to people. Some have poisonous bites or stings, like ants and wasps. Others are bloodsucking parasites, and as they drink their meals, they spread the tiny microbes that cause disease. These harmful insects tend to live in the world's warmer places.

A wasp's bright colors advertise danger.

RIVERS AND LAKES
Giant water bug

INSECT BODIES

An adult insect is fairly easy to recognize. It has three main parts—head, thorax, and abdomen. The thorax usually has six legs and two or four wings. But there are endless variations on this simple plan.

COMPOUND EYE
Insects have compound eyes made of many separate rod-shaped units called ommatidia. Each one sees a tiny part of the scene. These views are combined for an overall view. See cross section.

Cornea
Rhabdome
Lens
Optic nerve to brain

Heart
Brain
Crop

BODY CASING
Most insects have a tough body casing called the cuticle. This protects the soft inner parts such as the guts, muscles, and blood vessels. The muscles are attached to the inside of the cuticle and move the legs, wings, mouth, and other parts. So the insect's body casing is also its skeleton. Because it is on the outside, it is called an exoskeleton.

Coxa

Trochanter

MOUTHPARTS
The mouthparts of different insects are adapted to their particular food. Mouthparts may resemble sponges, suckers, scissors, or hollow needles. A bee's mouthparts include jaws that open and close from side to side, like pincers. Its long tongue laps up nectar, the sweet liquid in flowers.

A bee takes nectar from a flower

BRAIN AND NERVES
The main nerve from the brain is along the underside of the body. It has lumps, known as ganglia, which coordinate different sets of muscles.

Femur

LEGS
Each leg has a short coxa and trochanter, a femur and tibia, and a clawed foot or tarsi.

Tibia

Tarsi

MAIN PARTS

Thorax

Abdomen

Head

Legs and wings join to thorax

An insect's head is the center of its senses, with eyes, tasting mouthparts, and antennae that detect scent and movement. The thorax bears legs and wings. The abdomen contains mainly the parts for digestion, waste disposal, and breeding.

WINGS
Most adult insects have two pairs of wings. Muscles inside the thorax pull on its roof to flick the wings up and down.

HEART AND BLOOD
The heart is a tube near the top of the thorax. It pumps blood into a long upper vessel and around the thorax and abdomen.

Air sac

Spiracles

Trachea

Main nerve

Mid gut

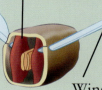

Vertical muscles pull, and roof "snaps" down.

Wings flick up.

Horizontal muscles pull, and roof goes up.

Wings flick down.

BREATHING
Air passes through holes called spiracles along the sides of the body and into tubes, or trachea.

DIGESTION
Food passes into the baglike crop for storage. It goes next to the midgut, where it is digested and where nutrients are taken into the body. Waste is stored in the hindgut before removal.

TOXIC BLOOD
Insects such as ladybugs have poisonous or toxic blood. Predators soon learn to recognize the insects' bright warning colors and leave them alone.

ANCIENT INSECTS

Insects were among the first animals to crawl on land, and as far as we know, the first to fly through the air. This all happened millions of years ago.

INSECT FOSSILS

We know about ancient life from fossils. These are the remains of animals and plants preserved in rocks or turned to stone. Most insects are small, and their bodies soon decay. So insect fossils are not as common as those of bigger animals with hard bones and teeth, like dinosaurs.

The earliest insect fossils are from about 350 million years ago. Life was spreading from the water and onto land, and insects were among the first of the new land creatures. They were the size of small ants and similar to the insects today called springtails.

DANGEROUS SWAMPS

Even 300 million years ago, insects were prey for other land animals. Big newtlike amphibians and early lizardlike reptiles stalked and hunted them.

MEGANEURA

This prehistoric dragonfly was a giant compared to today's types. Its wingspan was nearly 2 feet (60 centimeters).

INTO THE AIR

By 300 million years ago, insects had taken to the air. The climate was warm and wet, and much of the land was swampy. Flitting between the huge ferns were giant dragonflies, and scuttling among their stems were ancient cockroaches. Many other kinds of insects have come and gone since. Butterflies, bees, and other familiar insects started to appear when flowers began, about 100 million years ago.

LITTLE CHANGE

Today's cockroaches (above) and dobsonflies (right) are similar to their prehistoric cousins. Dobsonflies first appeared more than 250 million years ago, just before the dinosaurs. Some had wingspans of 8 inches (20 cm).

ENCASED IN AMBER

Amber is the dried, hardened juice, or resin, that oozes from certain plants, especially evergreen trees. Sometimes small creatures became stuck in the resin. The liquid continued to flow and cover them before it turned hard. Many insects, such as this lacewing, have been wonderfully preserved in every tiny detail inside lumps of amber.

DRAGONFLIES TODAY

Like its ancient ancestor, a modern dragonfly cannot fold its wings back. It usually holds them straight out and to the sides. Studying such details in living insects gives many clues about the way they have evolved.

Dragonfly wings are held out at rest.

POWER OF FLIGHT

Only three groups of animals are true masters of the air: bats, birds, and insects. Wings are one reason for the insects' success, allowing them to escape danger and to travel widely for food or mates.

FAST FLIER

Dragonflies are among the fastest insects. They can reach 37.5 miles (60 kilometers) per hour in short bursts, as they dart after small prey.

FOUR WINGS

Most insects have two pairs of wings. However, in some types, only one pair is used for flying. This is usually the rear pair. The front wings are smaller and harder and protect the rear pair, as in most grasshoppers and cockroaches. In beetles these front wings are fully hardened and cover the rear pair of wings and most of the body, too. These stiff wings are called elytra.

BEETLE FLIGHT

As a metallic wood-boring beetle takes off, it raises its colorful, hard wing cases and holds them out of the way. Then the rear pair of transparent wings can unfold fully for flight.

WING-BEAT SPEEDS

Large butterflies, such as swallowtails, flap their wings as slowly as four times each second. Some tiny gnats and midges can beat their wings more than 1,000 times every second. The speed of a bee's wings is 180 to 220 beats per second. This flapping makes the bee's buzzing sound.

HOOKED WINGS

On each side of a wasp's body, the front and rear wings are linked together by a hook structure. This enables the wings to flap together as one.

FLIGHT POWER

Wings are flapped by powerful muscles in the thorax. "Primitive" insects like dragonflies and cockroaches use a direct system where the muscles run from the thorax wall to the base of each wing. More "advanced" insects like flies, butterflies, beetles, and bees use the indirect system, where the muscles pull on the thorax itself.

In most insects, the wing is made of a very thin, see-through membrane stiffened by a branching pattern of small tubes called veins. Each vein contains a very thin blood vessel, nerve, and trachea (air tube).

Birdwing butterfly

Enlarged scales

SCALY WINGS

Butterflies and moths are Lepidoptera, which means "scaly wing." Thousands of microscopic scales cover the wings like fine powder, producing colors and patterns.

BALANCERS

Dipterans, or "true flies," have one working pair of wings. The rear pair, called halteres, are shaped like tiny drumsticks and swivel very fast to help provide balance. True flies include gnats, houseflies, and the cranefly (above).

LONGEST WINGS

The insects with the greatest wingspans are certain butterflies and moths. They include the Queen Alexandra's birdwing butterfly from Papua New Guinea, the Hercules moth of Australia and New Guinea, and the Atlas moth from Southeast Asia. They have wingspans of about 11 to 12 inches (28 to 30.5 cm). The *Megaloprepus* dragonfly has the longest wingspan of any dragonfly, at 7.5 inches (19 cm).

More than 10 kinds of birdwing butterflies are among the largest flying insects.

15

LEGS AND MORE LEGS

Insects have six legs each, but not always for the whole of their lives. The young of flies and beetles are known as maggots and grubs, and many of them have no legs at all.

LEGS WITH JOINTS

Insects, spiders, and similar animals are arthropods, which means "jointed legs." An insect leg has six to nine sections, like hollow tubes, linked by flexible joints. Muscles inside the tubes move the leg, which is joined to the thorax.

LEAP AND FLY

Grasshoppers, crickets, and locusts make enormous leaps by "unfolding" their rear legs. The legs straighten in two stages of movement, flinging the insect into the air.

"PRAYING" FOR PREY

Praying mantises have front legs that fold together, like a person praying. Each leg has a row of spines and folds back on itself like a jackknife to hold prey such as flies.

ON THE MOVE

Most insects use their six legs to move around. However, they do so in many different ways. In cockroaches, beetles, and ants, all six legs are about the same size, and these insects walk and run. In grasshoppers, crickets, and fleas, the third or rearmost pair of legs is much larger and more powerful than the other two pairs. These insects move in great leaps or jumps. A flea can leap higher than 100 times its own height.

Some insects use their legs to catch food, like the mantis. A dragonfly's legs dangle below its body in flight. They form a "basket" for trapping tiny prey such as gnats and midges in midair.

SHOVELING LEGS

The mole cricket's front legs are wide like shovels. The male cricket digs a burrow where he chirps to attract a female. Then the female digs a chamber to lay her eggs.

LEGS FOR SWIMMING

In water-dwellers such as diving beetles and backswimmers, the legs are broad with fringes of bristly hairs. The legs work like paddles, letting the insect row itself quickly through the water.

The great diving beetle's rear legs work like bristly oars.

SPECIALIZED LEGS

Not all insect legs are adapted for walking or running. The louse, a bloodsucking pest, has hook-shaped legs. These are poorly designed for running, but excellent for grasping and clinging to the hairs, fur, or skin of other creatures. Other insect legs have surprising abilities. The legs of a fly work well for walking, but also for tasting. Tiny taste sensors are scattered over the fly's feet. When the fly lands on a substance, it knows at once if that substance is suitable to eat or likely to be harmful.

SILVERFISH

This silverfish has the typical insect leg design of six slim limbs for walking and running. The legs move as two sets of three to keep the body well supported.

INSECT SENSES

Sight, hearing, smell, taste, and touch. Insects have the same main senses that we do. However, some of their sensing organs work very differently from our own.

EYES AND SIGHT

Most insects have both simple and compound eyes. A compound eye has many separate sections, ommatidia, that work together to form a fractured view, like a mosaic. This does not give insects a very clear view of their surroundings, but it does enable them to sense even very small movements.

LONG-HORNED BEETLE
The "horns" of the long-horned beetle are extra-long antennae. These beetles often move about at night, waving their antennae and tapping objects to find their way in the dark.

HEARING

Most insects can hear, but in a limited way. Their "ears" are patches of thin, flexible, skinlike cuticle. These are found in different places on different insects. For example, they are on the knees of grasshoppers and on the abdomen of cockroaches. Often these ears detect only the mating calls of the insect's own kind.

'BUG' EYES
The surfaces of the tiny units, or ommatidia, that make up an insect's compound eye can just be seen as shiny dots on this fly's (left) bulging eyes.

USEFUL ANTENNAE

In many insects, the antennae, or feelers, combine several senses. They can feel objects by direct touch and respond to the tiniest movements and vibrations. They can detect wind and water currents. Antennae sense odors floating in the air, especially from prey, enemies, or partners at breeding time. They can also taste.

As in other creatures, an insect's senses are adapted to its habitat and lifestyle. The antennae of a blind cave cricket may be three times the length of its body. They are extremely sensitive to touch, smell, taste, and tiny vibrations in the air caused by creatures moving nearby in the dark.

SCENTS FOR MATING

At breeding time, some kinds of insects, usually females, give off special scents called pheromones. These drift in the air, and are detected by males of the same species. The male follows the scent to find the female. Some male moths can detect a female from more than 2 miles (3.2 km) away.

A male moth's pheromone-detecting antennae

CHIRPING GRASSHOPPER

A male grasshopper or cricket chirps to attract a female at breeding time. The sounds are picked up by vibrating patches of thin cuticle on the female's knee joints or abdomen. These patches respond to very few other sounds.

19

CAMOUFLAGE—OR NOT

Being colored, patterned, and shaped to blend in with the surroundings is known as camouflage. Many insects are camouflaged, but others are meant to be noticed.

FEATURES OF CAMOUFLAGE

Two of the main features of camouflage are color and pattern. Bright green insects tend to live among fresh young leaves. Brown ones usually dwell among old, dead leaves and soil. Shape is also important in camouflage. Leaf insects have wide, green, leaf-shaped body parts, while their close cousins the stick insects, or "walking sticks," have slim, brown, twig-shaped bodies and legs.

PLANT IMPERSONATORS

Leaf insects and stick insects (inset) belong to the insect group known as the Phasmatodea. Even their eggs are shaped and colored to look like plant seeds.

BEHAVIOR

Another feature of camouflage is behavior. When the wind blows, stick and leaf insects tilt and sway with the twigs and leaves around them. Insects resembling flowers, thorns, or buds stay still when other animals are near.

LIVING THORN

Thorn bugs crouch down onto twigs or branches so that they resemble spiky thorns. Most of them feed by sucking up plant juices.

NOT VERY APPETIZING

Most animals avoid animal droppings, so the bird-dropping caterpillar is usually left alone.

Some insects have bright colors, even though they are not harmful or foul-tasting. They are known as mimics, because they mimic or copy the real advertising colors of similar insects. The viceroy butterfly is a mimic of the monarch, which really does have bitter-tasting flesh. The viceroy gains protection from its mimicry.

Birds and similar predators avoid the bad-tasting monarch butterfly.

The viceroy closely resembles the monarch.

FLASHY COLORS

Some insects use the opposite strategy to avoid predators. Their bright colors and patterns stand out. Usually these insects have horrible-tasting flesh, give off foul-tasting fluids, or are covered with stinging hairs. After a predator has had an encounter with these types of prey, it learns to recognize the coloration and leave the flashy creatures alone.

ALERT— I TASTE TERRIBLE!

Red, orange, and yellow are common advertising colors, often in combination with black or white. Some caterpillars increase the effect by rearing up in defense.

WHAT A STINK!

Some types of stinkbug ooze a bitter-tasting, horrible-smelling fluid when they are in danger. Their bright colors advertise this ability.

HUNTERS

Some kinds of insects are insectivores. This means they hunt, kill, and consume other insects. These predators use all kinds of tactics to capture prey, from sheer strength to stealth.

QUICK AND DEADLY

The main groups of hunting insects are dragonflies and damselflies, mantids, lacewings, alder flies and dobsonflies, and certain kinds of bugs, beetles, flies, wasps, and ants. The most skilled hunters in the air are dragonflies, which catch midges, gnats, and other small fliers.

Some dragonflies are darters. They watch from a perch and then dart out to grab passing prey. Others are hawkers, cruising regularly along their patch of territory, such as a riverbank, in search of food. The young or nymph dragonflies live in ponds and streams. They are also fierce and deadly, hunting worms, tadpoles, and young fish.

SUCKED TO DEATH

The insects called hemipterans, or "true bugs," include many hunting types. Assassin bugs hold down prey with their strong front legs and suck blood and fluids through their beaklike mouths.

PREDATORY CHASER

Darter dragonflies like this brown Libellula *cling to a reed, twig, or other convenient perch (like this rope) as they watch for prey.*

FATAL FLOWER

A flower mantid crouches among petals, waiting for small creatures. Then it grabs them with its spiky front legs.

SPIDER FOR DINNER

Most wasp young, or larvae, eat the bodies of other animals. The adult spider-hunting wasp stings and paralyzes its victim. It then places the spider into a nest or cell, where its young will hatch and eat the victim alive.

KING OF THE POND

The great diving beetle is the largest hunting insect in many ponds. It swims fast with its oarlike rear legs as it pursues small fish, tadpoles, and the young, or larvae, of other insects, such as flies. It grabs and tears up prey with its large jawlike mandibles. These beetles fly well and travel from pond to pond, usually at night.

The female great diving beetle has grooves along her back.

PHYSICAL AND CHEMICAL

Not all hunting insects need to be big. Some of their prey, like the tiniest insects and soil creatures such as eelworms, are as small as the period at the end of this sentence. The predatory insects that hunt them, such as certain kinds of wasps and beetles, would fit into this "o."

Some hunting insects have chemical weapons rather than physical ones such as big jaws. Hunting wasps have stingers with powerful chemicals that kill or paralyze their victim. Some of these wasps are able to attack other fierce hunters like centipedes, scorpions, or spiders that are 10 times their size.

PLANT-EATERS

Almost every part of every plant is food for insects somewhere in the world. Not only leaves, flowers, fruits, and seeds, but also roots, stems, bulbs, buds, bark, thorns, sap, and even solid wood.

ATTRACTED BY NECTAR

This swallowtail or papilionid butterfly has unrolled its long proboscis, which it uses like a drinking straw to sip nectar from a clover flower.

LEAFY MEALS

Leaves are very nutritious, especially when they are new, soft, and juicy. Caterpillars of butterflies and moths, the grubs of beetles, and the caterpillarlike larvae of sawflies can devastate whole forests in a few days.

LIQUID LUNCHES

Many plant-eating insects consume liquid meals such as sap. Some flowers make a sugary, syruplike liquid called nectar. This attracts insects such as butterflies, moths, beetles, flies, and bees. A butterfly or moth sucks the nectar through its long tubelike mouth, the proboscis. This is coiled up under the head when not in use. As the insects feed, their bodies become dusted with pollen grains from the flower. The insects then carry the pollen to other flowers of the same species, and the flower can then develop seeds.

MUNCH, MUNCH

Grasshoppers, locusts, and crickets like this spiny katydid (bush cricket) have toothlike mandibles that move from side to side to cut off pieces of leaves.

BIG MENU

Most kinds of earwigs (above) and cockroaches (below) are omnivores— they eat animals and plants. They chew most kinds of plant matter, from soft petals to hard bark. They also kill tiny creatures or feed on the bodies of dead animals.

EATING UNDERGROUND

The grubs of many beetles and flies live in soil for a year or two. They munch on plant roots until they change into adults. The young, or nymphs, of some types of cicadas suck juices from roots with their piercing mouthparts. They stay underground for 17 years before emerging as adults.

LEATHERJACKET

Tough-coated leatherjackets are larvae of the crane fly. They eat roots of crops and can be pests in farmland.

GALL WASPS

Some kinds of wasp larvae live and feed inside plants. They suck juices or eat tunnels into the stems of buds, leaves, or fruits. The plant responds by forming a hard lump or swelling, called a gall, around each larva. Different kinds of wasps cause different types of galls, such as oak-apple, spangle, or marble galls. As the larva grows into an adult, it eats its way out, leaving a tiny hole.

Most gall wasps are very tiny and lay their eggs only on one kind of plant.

PARASITES AND PESTS

The animals that cause most suffering and death in the world are not big predators such as tigers and sharks. They are insects that spread terrible diseases such as malaria and sleeping sickness.

BLOODSUCKERS

A parasite is a living thing that obtains food and shelter from another living thing, the host. The parasite usually harms the host in the process. Some kinds of insects are parasites to people and animals, especially bloodsuckers such as mosquitoes, fleas, lice, and bedbugs.

SWOLLEN WITH BLOOD

A female mosquito has hollow needlelike mouthparts that she jabs into the skin of people and animals to suck blood. She uses the blood, which swells her abdomen like a red balloon, to make eggs.

DISEASE SPREADERS

Malaria is passed on by *Anopheles* mosquitoes. As the female sucks blood from a person with malaria, she takes in some of the tiny *Plasmodium* organisms that cause the disease. When she bites the next person, the disease passes to that person. Tsetse flies spread sleeping sickness in a similar way.

WASP PARASITE ON A WASP

This ichneumon wasp pokes her sharp egg-laying tube, or ovipositor, into the mud nest of another kind of wasp. Her larvae will feed on the larvae of the host wasp.

Every few years, locusts breed and gather in the millions. In a few days, they can eat the food that would supply a townful of people for a year.

GERM-CARRIERS

Some insects spread germs in a more general way. Flies and cockroaches walk in dirt, on rotting plants and animals, and on animal droppings. They then wander across our floors, cooking utensils, kitchen countertops, and even our food. They spread illnesses such as typhoid and various types of food poisoning.

PESKY ROACH

Some cockroaches are known for infesting kitchens, especially in warmer climates. They feed mainly at night. When the light comes on, they race off to hide in cracks and corners.

CROP DAMAGE

Fields of farm crops are like feasts for some plant-eating insects such as locusts. The young of certain moths, flies, bugs (hemipterans), beetles, and weevils are also pests. With lots of food and good weather, they breed quickly and can eat a whole field in days. Pests like these damage all kinds of crops, from carrots and cabbages to rice, barley, and apples. Each year this causes millions of people to go hungry, especially in the world's tropical regions.

"KILLER BEES"

Honeybees are useful insects, and throughout many centuries, they have been bred to sting less often. In 1957 in South America, some fierce, more aggressive African bees were bred with local bees to try and increase their honey production. The resulting "killer bees" have spread through the Americas.

"Killer bees" defend their nests by stinging much more than ordinary honeybees.

FINDING A MATE

Insects breed in similar ways to other creatures. A female and male get together and mate, and the female lays eggs. The ways insects find and choose mates are varied and fascinating.

GREEN GLOW
So-called glowworms are really beetles. The wingless female makes a pulsing light on her lower abdomen to attract winged males, who then fly to her.

ATTRACTING A PARTNER
Most insects do not live with lots of others of their own species. So as the breeding season begins, they often need to attract a partner from a distance. Butterflies have bright colors and patterns to catch the attention of mates. Male grasshoppers, crickets, and cicadas make loud chirping or buzzing sounds to attract females. Many kinds of insects, usually females, give off special mating scents called pheromones. Males detect these scents with their antennae.

LONG-DISTANCE SCENT
Scents travel far. This is especially important in forests where sights and sounds work over limited distances. Male insects like this robin moth have feathery antennae to detect the pheromones released by females often hundreds of yards away.

DANGER!

In most kinds of mantises, the female is much larger than the male. He must approach with great caution, or she may eat him. He often gives the female a "present" of freshly killed prey to distract her while he gets on with mating.

COURTSHIP

Once a female and male insect meet, they often carry out courtship. This is usually a series of actions to check that the other is the right species, a suitable, healthy mate, and of the opposite sex. Courtship can involve displaying colors, flapping wings, stroking antennae, stomping feet, or giving off scents.

FEMALE-ONLY BREEDING

Some kinds of female insects, such as certain aphids, stick insects, mayflies, and wasps, can produce young without a mate. The young are clones of their mothers. This means that they have identical genes. This is known as parthenogenesis. It usually happens when conditions are very good, to build up numbers extremely quickly.

COMPETING FOR A FEMALE

Sometimes two or more members of the same sex, usually males, battle over one partner. Male stag beetles "wrestle" with their huge mandibles, or jaws. The muscles that move the mandibles are so weak that they rarely harm each other.

During parthenogenesis a female aphid does not lay eggs, but gives birth to tiny young.

GROWING UP

Different kinds of insects grow up in very different ways. Some hatch from their eggs as small versions of their parents and gradually get bigger. Others hatch looking completely different and must go through several stages of development.

ANT "EGGS"

In an ant nest, the eggs are kept clean and turned regularly by workers. The eggs hatch into maggotlike larvae that are fed by workers. Then the larvae become hard-cased pupae, often sold as ant "eggs" for aquarium fish to eat.

SLIGHT CHANGE OF SHAPE

The first type of growth, where the insect grows without changing its body shape very much, is known as incomplete metamorphosis. It happens in mayflies and dragonflies, grasshoppers and crickets, bugs, cicadas, and aphids. The young are called nymphs. They grow in stages by molting, or shedding, their tough, outer-body casing. The newly exposed casing is soft for a while so the insect must grow quickly before it hardens.

NYMPHS

Nymphs, like these stinkbug young (above left), have the same general shape as adults (above right), but they are smaller and may have different colors. Young stinkbug wings are small and useless at first but gradually grow in size (left).

EXTRA STAGE

Mayflies have an unusual extra stage in their lives, the subadult or subimago. They emerge from the water-dwelling nymph stage with wings but are unable to mate. It is not until after a final molt that they become adults.

TOTAL CHANGE OF SHAPE

The second type of growth, where body shape changes greatly during development, is called complete metamorphosis. It occurs in butterflies and moths, beetles, true (two-winged) flies like houseflies, and in bees, wasps, and ants. The eggs hatch into larvae, which are the main feeding stage. These larvae have different common names. Butterfly and moth larvae are called caterpillars, flies are called maggots, and beetle larvae are called grubs.

MASS PRODUCTION

In a beehive, larvae live in six-sided "boxes" called cells. They are fed on a mixture of half-digested nectar and pollen, which each worker bee brings up from its stomach.

Complete metamorphosis has four main stages. First is the egg, usually laid near a source of food. From this hatches a larva. It is active, eats hungrily, and molts several times. Then it forms a hard body case like a shell and becomes an inactive pupa. But inside, the body parts change greatly. Finally the pupal case splits open and the adult insect emerges.

A butterfly's eggs hatch into larvae called caterpillars ①. These are "eating machines" and grow quickly as they devour plant foods ②. After five molts in 10 to 14 days, the caterpillar becomes a hard-shelled pupa, called a chrysalis ③. Two weeks later, the adult or imago, like the monarch butterfly below, crawls out ④.

31

LIVING TOGETHER

Sometimes many insects gather together, such as flies on a dead animal. But they do not truly live together, they are just sharing food. The main insects that live with others of their own species are the termites, and hymenopterans (bees, wasps, and ants).

HORNETS

Hornets build a rounded nest, sometimes as large as a basketball, containing 2,000 or more members. The hornets use their powerful jaws to chew wood into a paperlike material that forms the nest.

SOCIAL INSECTS

These "social" insects usually live together in a nest, and they also work for each other. Every member of the group, or colony, has its own tasks, which it does for the good of the whole nest. The biggest member is usually the queen. Her task is to lay hundreds or thousands of eggs every day.

The queen is cared for by workers, who are smaller females that are unable to breed. In some colonies, different workers do different jobs, like cleaning the nest, caring for the young, or gathering food. In other groups, like honeybee colonies, each worker takes a turn at all the jobs.

TERMITE MOUND

A termite nest is below ground. Above ground, the tiny workers build a towering mound from soft mud that hardens in the sun. It helps to protect and cool the nest.

MARCHING ARMIES

Most social insects have nests that last a long time. They can last for more than 100 years. But army and driver ants of the tropics regularly move around. They stop for a few days in one place and catch all the prey they can. Then they go "on the march" again, destroying any creature who gets in their way.

A large colony of army ants can contain more than 1 million individuals. However, some termite nests are home to 10 times as many.

DEFENSE AND BREEDING

If the nest is attacked, workers rush to its defense. Many of them face certain death in order to protect the other workers, who are all their sisters. Some colonies of termites and ants have soldiers whose job it is to guard the nest. These are large workers with bigger jaws.

In most colonies, only a few members are male. These kings or drones do little except mate with the queen.

The nests made by social insects are some of the most complicated structures built by any animals, with different areas for the queen, rearing young, and storing food.

WAYS TO COMMUNICATE

Social insects communicate by touching antennae and by passing chemical messages, called pheromones, around the nest or hive.

UNSEEN TRAIL

Foraging ants lay a trail of invisible chemicals, or pheromones, which workers use to find food. Leaf-cutter ants take leaf pieces back to the nest and grow fungus on them to eat.

LONG-DISTANCE TRAVELERS

Why are some insects similar to certain whales, birds, and fish? Because they migrate, or go on regular, long-distance journeys, usually "there and back again" each year.

GOING NORTH

Each generation of monarchs flies hundreds of miles north, then produces young (right). Offspring mature and continue the journey.

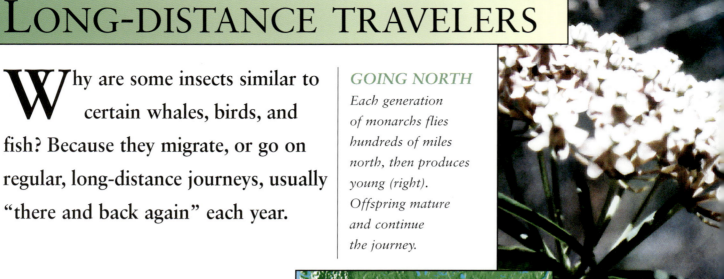

WHY TRAVEL?

Conditions around the world vary with the seasons. Summer in the far north brings extra sunlight and plant growth, but winter is dark and bitterly cold. One survival strategy is to travel north for summer, where there are fewer competitors for food, then return south to milder, easier conditions for winter. The best-known insect migrants, North America's monarch butterflies, do this. As they fly north, they breed, passing through up to five life generations or cycles. The return trip is carried out by a single generation of adults.

GOING SOUTH

Single monarchs on the southward trip fly more than 2,750 miles (4,400 km). They may find their way by sensing the sun's direction and the Earth's magnetic field.

REST THROUGH THE WINTER

About 5 million monarchs gather at 45 winter roosts, or resting sites, on trees in coastal California. Another 100-plus million roost at about 11 sites in upland central Mexico.

WINTER IN THE MOUNTAINS

Californian ladybugs partly fly and are partly blown to the Sierra Nevada's forests.

OCCASIONAL TRAVEL

Many kinds of butterflies and moths, and certain other insects, such as ladybugs, migrate like monarchs in a regular yearly pattern (although not so far). Another kind of mass movement is caused when the numbers of a species, such as locusts, rise greatly. This is usually because of good conditions but if numbers get too high the insects will quickly run out of food. They then have to set off to look for more food elsewhere.

SPRING IN THE VALLEYS

By early spring, the winds reverse and carry millions of winter-rested ladybugs back to the warm plains of California for breeding.

PLAGUES OF LOCUSTS

African locusts usually live alone in the dry northern regions. But if plentiful rains encourage plant growth, the locusts breed quickly and their offspring gather into swarms. If rains come again soon, numbers increase further. Giant swarms of 50 billion locusts fly off to find fresh food. They invade new areas and devastate farm crops over vast areas.

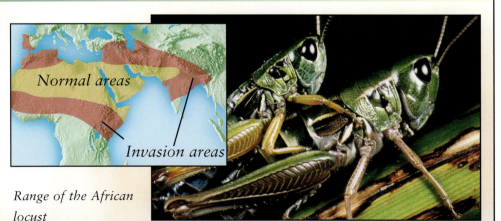

Normal areas

Invasion areas

Range of the African locust

When conditions are poor, locusts feed alone and come together only to mate (above). But after a good season, their coloring and behavior change. The offspring are bright yellow, orange, and black (left), and they gather together in swarms to feed.

FOREST INSECTS

Trees are like giant feasts for all kinds of plant-eating, or herbivorous, insects. In turn, these herbivores become food for their predatory cousins. A whole food web based on insects can build up around just one tree.

IN THE RAIN FOREST

Tropical rain forests have more species of plants and creatures than anywhere else on Earth. And more than 95 percent of animal species here are insects. Beetles, bugs, stick and leaf insects, termites, and many others eat almost every part of every tree. In turn, the insects are eaten by frogs, lizards, birds, and mammals such as shrews. In this way, the insects are central to the web of forest life.

PLENTY FOR EVERYONE

The leaves of a species of tree may be eaten by more than 1,000 different kinds of insects. Some of the most damaging are the caterpillarlike larvae of sawflies (above). There could be 1 million of these larvae on one huge tree. They chomp the leaves with their powerful chewing mouthparts, and their droppings fall like rain on the ground below.

LOUDEST NOISE

Tree cicadas make the loudest noises of any insect. A single group can be louder than a jackhammer drilling a road.

Male cicadas buzz to attract females.

WEEVILS

Weevils are a subgroup of beetles, with more than 50,000 species around the world. Most have a long "snout," or rostrum. Different species feed on various parts of trees, from sap to solid wood.

TREES' DEFENSE

A continuing "battle" occurs between trees and the insects eating them. Soft young buds and leaves emerge at about the same time each year. Leaf-eating insects also hatch around this time, to consume the young tree parts. Later, the leaves will develop poisonous substances, such as tannins, to protect the tree from insects.

GREEN SCARAB

Most forest insects are green (above) to merge with leaves, or brown (below) to blend with bark.

FOREST GIANTS

Tropical forests have the biggest insects. The Atlas moth has a wingspan of 1 foot (30 cm). Giant stick insects have bodies more than 1 foot (30 cm) long, and with legs held straight, their total length exceeds 20 inches (51 cm).

The Atlas moth of Southeast Asia

THE BATTLES CONTINUE

As blossoms open and seeds and fruits develop, there are similar "battles." The insects' life cycles are timed to take best advantage of their leafy hosts. In most years, both trees and insects succeed. Occasionally, unusual conditions mean more insects. Trees then take years to recover from the damage.

FRIGHTENING TWIG

Stick insects may suddenly spread their brightly colored wings to frighten away enemies.

"PEANUT HEAD"

Lantern flies are not true flies, but a type of bug (hemipterans). Also the strange peanut-shaped head does not glow like a lantern, as was believed. It is just brightly colored to attract a mate. Many lantern flies suck tree sap.

No insects live in the world's biggest habitat—the oceans. Yet many different kinds dwell in the fresh water of ponds, lakes, and rivers. Most do so only while young, or larvae, and leave when they reach adulthood.

BACKSWIMMER

Backswimmers (above) are predatory bugs like water striders (opposite). They feed in a similar way but from below the surface, sucking the prey's juice using a "beak."

THE NEED FOR AIR

Most insects breathe air, taken in through small holes along the sides of the body. A few underwater insects, such as the great diving beetle, use this system, too. So they must come to the surface regularly to obtain fresh supplies of air.

BREATHING BY GILLS

Most insects that stay below the surface breathe using gills. These are usually feathery-looking objects at the tail end or under the body. As blood flows through the gills, oxygen dissolved in the water seeps into it. The gills have a large surface area to take in plenty of oxygen. The nymphs of dragonflies, damselflies, and mayflies all breathe in this way.

POND RULER

In many small ponds, the dragonfly nymph is the top predator, catching small fish, tadpoles, and even young frogs.

WATER BUG

This fierce bug (right) has "jackknife" front legs, like those of a mantis, to grab prey. It lurks among water weeds and dashes out to ambush its victims.

WALKING ON WATER

Water striders are true bugs (hemipterans) specialized to skim or slide across the water's surface without sinking. Their legs are fringed with many small hairs that trap air and support their weight without breaking the surface. The front legs sense and capture tiny prey stuck in the surface. The middle pair of legs row like oars, and the rear pair are used for steering.

Water striders can jump and fly as well as skim.

PREDATORS AND PREY

Some underwater nymphs are hunters, like those of dragonflies and damselflies. They catch any small water creature they can overpower, including the nymphs of mayflies and stone flies, which eat plants. All of these nymphs spend between one and three years underwater, growing and shedding their body casings in the usual way. They then crawl up stems into the air, split their outer casings, and emerge as winged adults.

DOBSONFLY

The nymphs of dobsonflies live in water for a few years, turn into pupae, and then emerge as adults with wingspans of 6 inches (15 cm).

LAYING EGGS

A female damselfly lays her eggs in the stems of water plants, such as reeds.

SCRUB AND DESERT INSECTS

Deserts are among the harshest habitats because the lack of water causes enormous problems. But many insects, with their tough eggs and watertight body casings, can survive here.

FOOD AND WATER

Food is scarce in many scrub and desert regions. When they have little to eat, insects can simply slow down their body processes, become inactive, and take shelter in the rocks and sand. This is very different from birds and mammals, which are active and warm-blooded and need to eat regularly. In one year, a large beetle eats less than 1 percent of the food needed by a mouse of the same size.

Desert insects have life cycles suited to harsh and changing conditions. The tough-cased eggs survive scorching heat and long drought. When rains come and bring plant growth, the eggs hatch and the larvae have food.

DRINKING FOG

A darkling beetle raises its abdomen in the morning fog of the Namib Desert. It drinks the water drops that run down its body.

DUNG ROLLER

Animal droppings are valuable sources of moisture and nutrients in the desert. The dung beetle fashions a lump into a ball, rolls it away, digs a pit, puts in the ball, lays eggs on it, and covers it. When the larvae hatch, they have a delicious meal waiting for them.

JERUSALEM CRICKET

The dune cricket is very different from its forest dwelling relatives. Its pale body is camouflaged in the sandy soil. Its powerful limbs dig rapidly to find food and hide it from enemies.

ANT LIONS

Ant lions are related to lacewings and have similar large, lacy-looking wings. They hunt smaller insects and suck out the body juices with their sharp, hollow, tube-shaped mouthparts. The larva of the ant lion digs a cone-shaped pit in sandy soil and waits buried at the bottom. Small prey like ants slip and slide into the pit, and the larva grabs them with its large pincerlike jaws.

Adult ant lions resemble lacewings, but their antennae are longer and bent, or clubbed.

VELVET "ANT"

This hairy-looking "ant" is really a type of wasp. The wingless female races about on the ground, looking for the pupa of another wasp. She lays eggs in it, and her larvae eat the pupa alive.

MATING CALLS

As in other habitats, many desert beetles leave trails of special scent and tap the ground with their legs to attract a mate.

DAY AND NIGHT

Some insects are out by day in the desert, such as locusts and a few butterflies. But most come out only at night. They avoid the worst of the heat and being dried out by the sun. They can also avoid predators in the darkness. These nocturnal insects include many kinds of beetles, which sift through the sand for edible scraps.

BLISTER BEETLE

When attacked, types of blister or oil beetles ooze oily liquid that has a horrible taste and can cause skin blisters. Many of these lay their eggs in the larvae of other insects.

41

INSECTS AND US

Much of the web of life on earth depends on insects. They are predators, prey, and pollen-carriers in almost every land habitat. But they are also pests, harming us and our pets, farm animals, and crops.

INSECTS THAT HELP US

Insects are vital as the pollinators in our fruit orchards and vegetable fields. Predatory insects like ladybugs and lacewings catch smaller insects, such as aphids (blackfly and greenfly), and help keep these plant pests under control. Around the world, people regularly eat more than 500 kinds of insects, from crickets and termites to grubs and caterpillars. Other insects provide many useful products.

ESSENTIAL POLLINATORS

Butterflies, flies, bees, beetles, and many other insects carry pollen grains, helping flowers develop fruits and seeds. Without their work, we would grow far fewer tasty fruits and vegetables or beautiful garden flowers.

INSECT PRODUCTS

Bees make honey to feed their larvae, but we also take some for our use. Silkworms are really silk moth caterpillars. They spin cocoons around themselves, and we take the thread to make silk cloth. Shellac is a special varnish made from certain scale insects.

Shellac

Beehives

Silk

POTATO PEST

The Colorado potato beetle eats potato leaves. Like many pests, this insect has spread to new regions through food shipments.

INSECTS THAT CAUSE HARM

Flies and other insects carry germs that kill millions of people every year. Giant fields of crops, or huge stores full of fruits or grains, are massive meals for certain insects. We spray insecticide chemicals, but these kill non-pest insects, too, which are food for birds and other creatures. The damage spreads along the food chain and upsets the balance of nature.

The fruit fly *Drosophila* is attracted to old, moldy fruit—and is enormously important in science. It has been bred in the billions to study heredity—the way genes work and how they pass from parents to offspring. The flies are easy to keep, their life cycle lasts just 12 days, and they exist in many different genetic forms, or mutations.

The Oxford red variant of the fruit fly has large red eyes, caused by a mutated gene.

ROACH INFESTATION

This female cockroach is laying an egg case, or ootheca, containing about 30 eggs. One of the main reasons for insects' success is the speed at which they can breed. With short life cycles they build up vast numbers in just a few weeks.

ANIMAL CLASSIFICATION

The animal kingdom can be split into two main groups, vertebrates (with a backbone) and invertebrates (without a backbone). From these two main groups, scientists classify, or sort, animals further based on their shared characteristics.

The six main groupings of animals, from the most general to the most specific, are: phylum, class, order, family, genus, and species. This system was created by Carolus Linnaeus.

To see how this system works, follow the example of how human beings are classified in the vertebrate group and how earthworms are classified in the invertebrate group.

ANIMAL KINGDOM

VERTEBRATE	**INVERTEBRATE**
PHYLUM: Chordata	**PHYLUM:** Annelida
CLASS: Mammals	**CLASS:** Oligochaeta
ORDER: Primates	**ORDER:** Haplotaxida
FAMILY: Hominids	**FAMILY:** Lumbricidae
GENUS: *Homo*	**GENUS:** *Lumbricus*
SPECIES: *sapiens*	**SPECIES:** *terrestris*

ANIMAL PHYLA

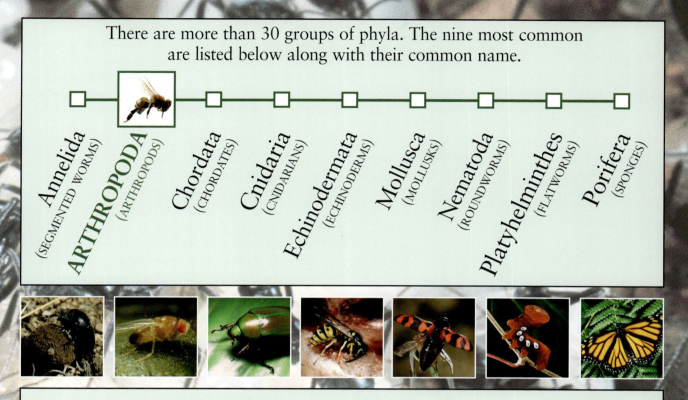

There are more than 30 groups of phyla. The nine most common are listed below along with their common name.

Annelida
(SEGMENTED WORMS)

ARTHROPODA
(ARTHROPODS)

Chordata
(CHORDATES)

Cnidaria
(CNIDARIANS)

Echinodermata
(ECHINODERMS)

Mollusca
(MOLLUSKS)

Nematoda
(ROUNDWORMS)

Platyhelminthes
(FLATWORMS)

Porifera
(SPONGES)

This book highlights animals from the Arthorpoda phylum. Follow the example below to learn how scientists classify the *viridula*, or southern green stink bug.

INVERTEBRATE

PHYLUM: Arthropoda

CLASS: Insecta

ORDER: Meteroptera

FAMILY: Pentatomidae

GENUS: *Nezara*

SPECIES: *viridula*

A southern green stink bug (viridula)

GLOSSARY

ABDOMEN
In an insect, the rearmost part of the body that usually contains parts involved in digesting food, getting rid of waste, and breeding

ANTENNAE
An insect's "feelers"—usually two long parts on the head that are sensitive to touch, smells, taste, and movements such as wind and water currents

ARTHROPODS
Invertebrates with exoskeletons and jointed legs; arthropods include insects, spiders, and scorpions

CAMOUFLAGE
The disguising of an animal by the way it is colored and patterned to blend or merge with its surroundings

COMPOUND EYE
An eye formed of many different parts or sections, called ommatidia, as found in insects and some similar creatures

CUTICLE
The outer layer or covering of an insect's body casing, which gives protection

ELYTRA
The hardened, stiff front pair of wings on a beetle that protect the second pair, which are used for flight

EVOLUTION
The change in living things through time as they become better adapted or suited to their surroundings or environment

EXOSKELETON
The body casing of an insect, with muscles attached on the inside, which acts as the body's supporting framework or skeleton

HABITAT
A particular type of surroundings or environment where plants and animals live, such as a desert, pond, or seashore

INSECTIVORE
An animal that eats mainly insects and other similar small creatures

LARVA
The second stage in the life of most insects, which hatches from the egg and is usually active as it moves around and eats; the plural of *larva* is *larvae*

LIFE CYCLE
The entire life of an animal or plant; in most insects it is divided into four main stages: egg, larva (or nymph), pupa, and adult

MANDIBLES
Jawlike mouthparts possessed by some insects

METAMORPHOSIS
Change in body shape during growing up or development

MIGRATION
A regular long journey, usually at the same time each year, to avoid harsh conditions such as cold or drought

MIMICRY
When an animal is not harmful or horrible-tasting but is colored and patterned to resemble another, the model, which is; predators avoid the mimic since it looks like the model

NECTAR
Sweet liquid made by flowers to attract insects and other creatures for pollination

NYMPH
The second or immature stage in the life of some insects; the nymph resembles the adult in general shape and form

PARASITE
An organism that satisfies a need such as food or shelter by living off another organism, called the host, and harms the host in the process

PARTHENOGENESIS
When a female animal produces young without having mated with a male

PHEROMONES
Scent chemicals given off by an insect that work as signals for communication with others of its kind

PUPA
The third stage in the life of some insects, after the larva and before adulthood; the plural of *pupa* is *pupae*

THORAX
In an insect, the middle part of the body that usually carries the legs and wings

SPIRACLES
Small holes along the sides of an insect's body that allow air into the system of breathing tubes or trachea

FURTHER RESOURCES

AT THE LIBRARY
Birch, Robin. *Mosquitoes Up Close.* Chicago: Raintree, 2005.

Maynard, Christopher. *Bugs: A Close-up View of the Insect World.* New York: Dorling Kindersley, 2001.

Miller, Sara Swan. *Ants, Bees, and Wasps of North America.* New York: Franklin Watts, 2003.

Robertson, Matthew. *Insects and Spiders.* Pleasantville, N.Y.: Reader's Digest Children's Books, 2000.

Squire, Ann. *Termites.* New York: Children's Press, 2003.

ON THE WEB
For more information on this topic, use FactHound.

1. Go to *www.facthound.com*
2. Type in this book ID: 0756512506
3. Click on the *Fetch It* button.

FactHound will find the best Web sites for you.

INDEX